# SLINGSHOT DRAGSTERS

## of the 1960s PHOTO ARCHIVE

Lou Hart

# Iconografix

### PHOTO ARCHIVE SERIES

Iconografix
PO Box 446
Hudson, Wisconsin 54016 USA

Library of Congress Control Number: 2005927240

ISBN-13: 978-1-58388-148-4
ISBN-10: 1-58388-148-4

05 06 07 08 09 6 5 4 3 2 1

Printed in China

Cover and book design by Dan Perry

Copyediting by Suzie Helberg

**Cover photo**- See page 117. *Photo by James Handy*

## BOOK PROPOSALS

Iconografix is a publishing company specializing in books for transportation enthusiasts. We publish in a number of different areas, including Automobiles, Auto Racing, Buses, Construction Equipment, Emergency Equipment, Farming Equipment, Railroads & Trucks. The Iconografix imprint is constantly growing and expanding into new subject areas.

Authors, editors, and knowledgeable enthusiasts in the field of transportation history are invited to contact the Editorial Department at Iconografix, Inc., PO Box 446, Hudson, WI 54016.

# Acknowledgments

I would like to thank each and every one whose contributions helped make this book possible, especially:

Al Nosse, for his photos from the early days at Detroit...

Jay, Karen, Mike, Ryan, Rie, Roger, Michelle, and Steve at Jack's Camera for their great service...

Bob Thompson's photographs, along with Paul Katata, for their countless hours of research and desire to help put this project together...

Tim Pearl and Dale Kunesh for their support and knowledge...

Steve and Marie Delgadillo for their photos and priceless research materials, along with their years of friendship...

Arthur W. Bombay's photography...

James Handy for whom without his work this book would have not been possible...

Rick Stewart, Roland Leong, Dennis Holding, Jim Crooke, Bob Muravez with Floyd Lippencott, Jr., Tommy Ivo, and Don Garlits for taking their valuable time sharing their moments on the Greatest Era of Drag Racing...

Tom "The Mongoose" McEwen; a very special "thank you" to one of the all-time legends of drag racing for his help and hospitality...

And to my son Brandon who didn't complain too much with this book that was sandwiched in-between doing father and son activities...

# Foreword by Tom McEwen

It's a real pleasure having the opportunity to write the foreword for Lou Hart's latest nostalgia project. This book will astonish and inform newcomers to drag racing and provide a trip back to the 'good old days' for the seasoned veterans of the dragster wars.

Touching on memories of a personal nature: My drag racing career began in 1953 at the Santa Ana, California drags, running my mom's late model Olds. If someone would have approached me in the staging lanes and predicted I'd achieve some degree of fame and fortune competing in the newly created sport, I'd have laughed in their face. Further, if they said the 'business office' I'd work out of for much of my career would be the thinly padded aluminum seat shrouded under a 'funny car' body…well, I'd start looking for security.

My first big break came in 1960 following the untimely death of Leonard Harris when I hooked up with Gene Adams and took over the reigns of the Albertson Olds which Leonard had so successfully driven. It was the baddest gas dragster ever to compete. Next Gene and I raced, again successfully, the 'High Back Gasser.' This beautifully designed 'Shark Car' followed, Gene ran it on gas, alcohol and nitro. We almost won the famed 'Smokers' Bakersfield meet with it. Our last project together was a featherweight creation Kent Fuller welded up, that I called the 'push rod' car, because of its small diameter chassis tubing. We ran Olds, Mickey Thompson Pontiacs and Chrysler hemis on gas and fuel in that little flyer.

Gene got tired of rebuilding all the stuff the nitro tore up and opted to return to gas competition, but I had 'tasted' the kick of nitromethane and wanted more, so we amicably parted ways.

My next 'dream ride' came in June of '64, when famed engine builder Ed Donovan chose me to drive the Donovan Engineering Special. A month later, one of the greatest and longest lasting rivalries in all of professional sports (not just motor sports) was born. After beating Don "The Snake" Prudhomme at a Pomona race, Donovan, who was fond of nicknames, christened me "The Mongoose," following my victory over "The Snake." "Just like in *The Jungle Book*," he shouted. The Mongoose versus The Snake.

I could smell a powerful promotional tool with this "Mongoose" name and I ran with it. First creating a fierce looking creature for my helmet, then set about building my persona. Pro wrestling was as big back in the '60s as it is now, and I quickly picked up on the fact that the 'bad guys' got most of the ink, so I chose to assume that role. The fans at Lions used to do everything but throw bottles at me when I raced there. I never missed an opportunity to take a jab at my opponents, especially in *Drag News*. Prudhomme came off as the good guy and me, bad to the bone. The racing press and the fans ate it up; as a matter of fact, they still do! Don and I will be tied together as long as drag racing carries on.

1965 marked by first experience (and almost my last) with a 'funny car' – the rear-engined Hemi-Cuda I. Several weeks after its debut, while making some shakedown passes at Lions, the flying fish literally took wing. Up, up and over several times. Race car aerodynamics was a whole new game, especially for the new wave of 'funny cars.' Instead of building a race car, we had inadvertently constructed an airplane wing. The air rushing over and under the car created lift, and off she went. Luckily I escaped uninjured. The lessons we learned the hard way were employed in the construction of Hemi-Cuda II, and it turned out to be a darned decent race car.

In addition to driving the Cuda I and II my main chore of this period in my career was driving the potent Yeakel Plymouth Top Fueler, owned by good friend Lou Baney. The Yeakel car morphed into the Brand Ford T/F which ended up as the famous Brand Overhead Cam Ford Dragster. Soon after the latter occurred, Lou and I had our parting of the ways.

After stints with Jerry Bivens and Don "The Beachcomber" Johnson in '67, the following year found me back, driving my own T/Fer...featuring my first non-automotive sponsor – Tirend Activity Booster. Toward the end of '68 I gave in to the rising tide of 'funny cars,' and bought the ex-Candies & Hughes Barracuda.

In '69 I hit the road on a national tour with both cars! Driving and maintaining a Top Fueler and a Nitro Funny Car, racing every week, some weeks with multiple appearances, now that was drag racing...old school.

1970 brought the 'revolution' to drag racing, complements of "The Mongoose," "The Snake," and Mattel toys. You might say I was the brains behind the deal and Don the brawn. He was totally focused on racing, but I saw the bigger picture of what would be necessary to pull this deal off.

No one had seen the likes of what we unleashed upon the sport. Big money, non-automotive sponsor, strong marketing and promotional backing, top of the line funny cars and equipment, crew uniforms and tricked-out car haulers. On paper Don and I were part-

ners, but when it came to racing one another, it was 'take no prisoners.' It didn't matter if it was the U.S. Nationals or a match race at some poorly lit track in the middle of an Ohio cornfield, we both raced to win. No team orders for us!

So now, let's set the year to 1960 in 'Way Back Machine' and relive drag racing's exciting past.

*Tom McEwen*

*Photo courtesy Tom McEwen*

# Introduction

Sling shot (slingshot) *n.* A Y-shaped stick having an elastic strap attached to the prongs, used for flinging small stones.

Slingshots, diggers, rails, fuelers, "Monsters of the Midway," or the "Kings of Smoke," by any name you would still have the Giants of the Quarter Mile: The Slingshot Dragsters!

Since its creation, the Top Fuel dragster is the quickest accelerating vehicle in motorsports. Although drag racing started back in the 1950s, man's fascination for speed began back in 1906, when Fred and Marriott Stanley, the inventors of the Stanley Steamer, built a wooden speedster propelled by steam. As Fred drove, the speedster accelerated to a speed of 127.66 mph. Tragedy struck when the speedster went airborne and crashed nose first into the ground, proving fatal for the brothers. Since then, hot rodders have been finding ways to go faster and quicker to see who has the "baddest" hot rod around!

The earliest dragster chassis consisted of steel in either tubular or squared form, a simple roll bar, engine, a seat mounted over the rear end, and seat belts, with rear drum brakes. From home built to production chassis, the dragster was getting more popular with each and every event.

Always looking for a way to have an edge up on the competition, innovators like Mickey Thompson developed lightweight chassis, engine parts, and components, and tested their durability. Also playing a roll were the fuels used by these beasts; pump gas, alcohol, nitromethane, and even the rocket fuel hydrazine, was being tested. As times got quicker and speeds increased, along with accidents, the safety issues were a cause for alarm. Disc brakes and parachutes were needed to slow the cars down. The NHRA banned the use of nitro, hydrazine, and other exotic fuels and additives. High octane pump gasoline was used in competition. Chassis were lengthened, larger engine displacements were increased, improved superchargers were developed, and soon NHRA lifted the ban on nitro and the competition levels increased.

Racing legend Don Garlits changed the face of drag racing. Known as "Big Daddy," Don has dominated the sport and has been the greatest influence in the development of the Top Fuel dragster. In 1963, Don developed and built a wing mounted over the driver's seat to make the dragster more aerodynamic. Don also built many versions of his Swamp Rat dragsters with refinements to the chassis and body for faster and quicker times. Don became the most feared racer in drag racing!

As the popularity of drag racing increased all over the U.S., drag racing turned to Hollywood to promote its product on the silver screen. In the *Bikini Beach* movie with Frankie Avalon and Annette Funicello, drag racers Tommy Ivo and Don Prudhomme displayed their talents with overwhelming success.

At most NHRA and AHRA national events, over 90 Top Fuel dragsters competed to make a 32-car field. For many owners and drivers, match racing was their bread and butter. Match racing allowed them to buy the extra parts needed to be competitive and allowed them to make a decent living. Fuel cars received a larger payout purse than gas dragsters, but Top Gas dragsters were also gaining in popularity. With a break on weight and engine combinations, gasoline was less hard on parts, and cheaper than nitro. Multiple engines could be used for increased horsepower and performance. For example, The *Freight Train* ran twin small-block supercharged Chevrolet engines, The *Odd Couple* ran a big-block supercharged Chrysler Hemi mated with a blown small-block Chevrolet engine, and Gordon Collect ran with twin supercharged Chrysler Hemis.

Many drivers achieved success, but one particular driver had to hide his identity due to the fact that his family insisted he quit driving and concentrate more on the family business. Bob Muravez, the driver of the *Freight Train* Top Gas dragster, won several national events. Bob attended the events but only as a crewmember. During a period of a few months, the *Train* failed to qualify for several races, so Bob climbed back into the cockpit and set a low elapsed time at the races, which he easily won! To keep his identity from the newspapers, track announcers Steve Gibbs and Mel Rick gave Bob the name Floyd Lippencott, Jr. Trophy photos taken of Bob showed him without removing his facemask. After winning a national event, Bob jumped from the cockpit and switched places with certain crewmen so that the crewman got to kiss the trophy girl, have their photo taken, and receive the trophy, as Bob was seen off to the side with a smile on his face!

Purse money, along with contingency awards, was increasing to record highs with bonus money paid for national records of elapsed times and speeds. More durable parts were developed with stronger and lighter metals. Aerodynamic body changes made the dragster gain higher miles per hour at quicker low elapsed times.

In March 1970 at Lions Drag Strip in Long Beach, Don Garlits suffered a clutch explosion that cut his car in two and severed a part of his right foot. Don was out of racing for nearly a year but returned in 1971 with his mid-engine Top Fuel dragster. After receiving a bag of mixed reviews, Garlits swept nearly every National event he entered in 1971, setting record low elapsed times and speeds as he dominated in almost every Top Fuel category. Don changed the history of drag racing, thus ending an era of front motor dragsters.

Several legends of the "Slingshot" were able to share memorable times with me of this fantastic era in drag racing history. I wish to thank Rick Stewart, Roland Leong, Bob Muraverz, aka Floyd Lippencott, Jr., Don Garlits, Tommy Ivo, and Tom McEwen for their contributions to this book. I'm overwhelmed that I received the opportunity to work with these gracious legends of the quarter mile. I hope you'll enjoy it!

Lou Hart

The Knapp-Westerdale #362 dragster launchs at the 1960 NHRA Detroit Nationals. Westerdale, who eventually went on to drive for the Ramchargers, drove the twin-V Chevy. *Al Nosse*

The *Bad News* slingshot dragster blasts down the quarter mile at the 1960 Detroit Nationals. Chassis Research built the car. It was fitted with a small-block fuel-injected Chevy engine. *Al Nosse*

The 1961 NHRA Nationals was moved to its permanent home in Clermont, Indiana. Mickey Thompson is driving his *Tempest* dragster. It featured a blown supercharged Pontiac four-cylinder motor. The half V-8 had the supercharger mounted on the left side of the motor. *Photo courtesy the scrapbook of Lou Hart*

Another Mickey Thompson creation at the 1961 Nationals was this conventional dragster powered by a super-charged Pontiac big-block engine. *Photo courtesy of the scrapbook of Lou Hart*

The Albertson Olds gas dragster of Gene Adams and Tom McEwen gave Tom the start in his successful driving career. Here, Tom blasts down the quarter mile at Bakersfield. *Photo courtesy of the scrapbook of Tom McEwen*

Another shot of Mickey Thompson's *Tempest* four-cylinder dragster gave Mickey a clear view down the track void of any obstructions. The engine was basically a stock 326 c.i. motor cut in two. The four-cylinder motor was fitted into production Pontiac Tempests and LeMans. *Photo courtesy of the scrapbook of Tom McEwen*

*Iron Mistress*, the twin-engine dragster of Bill Colburn and Neil Leffler, had two blown in-line Chrysler Hemis with two offset Halibrand quick-change differentials, and featured a fitted Messerschmitt body. *Photo courtesy of the scrapbook of Tommy Ivo*

Mickey Thompson's twin–V, four-wheel drive dragster featured twin blown Pontiac engines. The four-wheel drive produced a tremendous amount of torque, which caused four-wheel burnouts down the quarter mile. *Photo courtesy of the scrapbook of Tommy Ivo*

The South Bay Shifters Car Club of So. Cal., ran this popular but unusual steam-powered dragster at Lions Drag Strip. Steam bellowed from a special exhaust system found behind the driver's seat. Note that no safety measures were taken here, as the driver's seat wasn't fastened, and he wore only a tee shirt, and steam burns were a problem. The rear Halibrand wheels were mounted inside out and the top speed was just over 50 mph. *Lou Hart*

Mickey Thompson built this twin Pontiac-Olds-powered gas dragster. The white digger featured a crank-driven intake supercharger on the front engine with a belt-driven blower on the rear. Jack Chrisman drove the gas dragster after he won the first NHRA Championship driving the Howard Cams *Twin Bear*. *Lou Hart*

## Rick Stewart

*"We set numerous record wins, top speeds, and elapsed times with engine wizard Gene Adams. Being successful, we later sold the car to the 'Northwest King' Jerry Ruth."*

Rick "The Iceman" Stewart drove the Beacon Automotive Top Fuel dragster here at Lions Drag Strip at Long Beach, California. Gene Adams mastered the tune-ups from the blown 392 c.i. Chrysler Hemi that featured a Woody Gilmore chassis. The dragster ran constant 7-second times with speeds above 190 mph. Rick is currently the head starter for NHRA. *Lou Hart*

The Beacon Automotive Top Fuel dragster gets fitted with new blower pulleys and belt in-between rounds at Lions. Adams-Stewart were strong contenders on the West Coast circuit. *Lou Hart*

At Lions Drag Strip in Long Beach, the C-T Stroker *Black Beauty* Top Fuel dragster of Wenderski and Winkle featured an early Chrysler Hemi, a Tommy Ivo-built chassis, American Racing wheels, a Bob Sorrell body, and black and silver paint applied by Rick's Auto Body. "Big John" Wenderski drove the popular digger but an unfortunate accident at Ramona claimed his life. *Lou Hart*

Innovator Mickey Thompson built this blown Pontiac A-Fuel dragster using a Pontiac big-block engine and adapting hemispherical-type heads. Thompson and Jack Chrisman (shown looking in the cockpit) teamed up to campaign the Pontiac. *Lou Hart*

The team of Weekly, Rivera, Fox, and Holding, "The Frantic Four" A/Fuel dragster featured an Ivo-Peppmuller chassis, an early 335 c.i. Chrysler Hemi, Belanger headers, and upholstery by Don's Auto Upholstery. The Frantic Four ran consistent 8.20 e.t.'s of 190-plus mph. *Lou Hart*

George Cerney, Jr., drove and owned this popular modified roadster. Powered by a small-block 301 c.i. injected Chevrolet engine, the popular auto painter dominated the 3rd eliminator bracket at Lions Drag Strip running constant 9.70 e.t.'s with speeds over 145 mph. *Lou Hart*

Gordon "Collecting" Collett from Portsmouth, Ohio, passes time waiting to make a pass at Lions Drag Strip in Long Beach. A Scotty Fenn-built K-88 chassis, along with American Racing Wheels, Isky cams, and an early small-block Chrysler Hemi, provided the power on pump gas. *Lou Hart*

Rollema & Hill's blown Chevrolet small-block engine featured a GMC supercharger and chassis built by Joe Ithows with a torsion bar style front suspension, and unique air scoop intake system and fairings mounted in front of the rear slicks. *Lou Hart*

The blown Olds-powered dragster of Safford-Gaide-Ratican, "The Sour Sisters," ran consistent 8.09 e.t.'s with speeds over 191 mph. Kenny Safford drove the "world's quickest Olds" to the winner's circle several times throughout the west. *Lou Hart*

Drag racing legend the late Tony Nancy's *22 Jr.* dragster featured a Fuller-built chassis, a Cal Automotive 23T body, Halibrand wheels, and a blown-supercharged motor that ran on pump gasoline. Tony won the 1963 NHRA Winternationals in the Comp Eliminator class running an 8.96 e.t. of 170.18 mph. *Lou Hart*

At the 1963 NHRA Winternationals, Chris Karamesines' *Chizler* dragster had an early 392 c.i. Chrysler Hemi. Karamesines, known as "The Speed King from Chicago," was the first to break 200 mph at Alton, Illinois, in April 1960. Although it wasn't considered an official run, this was considered one of his greatest achievements. *Lou Hart*

Ed Schultz of Lompoc, California, spent $6,000 to build this first Class AA Fuel dragster using an Ivo chassis, a Reath Automotive built '57 Chrysler Hemi bored out to 400 c.i., a Reath chrome crank, and a 6-71 Delta blower drive on a Cragar manifold. Ed himself crafted the headers. Bob Sorrell hand formed the Ivo styled body with M&H slicks mounted on American Racing wheels. Dave McKenzie piloted the Ed's Muffler Top Fuel entry to an 8.12 e.t. – running 187 mph at the 1963 NHRA Winternationals at Pomona. *Lou Hart*

Prior to facing Connie Kalitta in the final round at the 1963 NHRA Winternationals at Pomona, John Peters straps in driver Bob Muravez in the Peters and Frank twin-engined Chevrolet Top Gas dragster. The Peters and Frank entry defeated Kalitta with an 8.82 e.t. of 178 mph. Muravez, whose identity was hidden, posed for photos in the winner's circle with his helmet left on. *Lou Hart*

Don Garlits' *Swamp Rat V* is shown here at the 1963 NHRA Winternationals at Pomona. Always the innovator, Don experimented with his ideas on his racecars. At Pomona he debuted with this radical wing above the driver, winning Top Eliminator at the Winternationals with a come-from-behind 8.25 e.t. 186.32-mph-blast to beat Art "The Dart" Malone. *Lou Hart*

This photograph of an unidentified dragster was taken at the 1963 Winternationals. The gas dragster was clean and simple. An early Chrysler Hemi pumped out approximately 800 horsepower on pump gas. *Lou Hart*

The dragster of the Graif Brothers sported a small-block Chrysler Hemi using an Engle camshaft. Driver Chuck Graif drove the gas dragster to mid 8.00 e.t.'s. *Lou Hart*

# Memorable Moments of the 1960s
## Tom McEwen

*"Bakersfield 1963 March Meet; Gene Adams and I with the Shark car faced off with "Big Daddy" Don Garlits - and HE'S the one to beat! We added 25 percent nitro to the fuel tank, fired up the car, and staged with him. As the light turned green I released the clutch and blasted to an 8.24 e.t. 181-mph-pass to defeat Swingle."*

Tom McEwen in the McEwen-Adams Top Fuel dragster battles it out with Connie Swingle in "Big Daddy" Don Garlits' *Swamp Rat III* at the 3rd Annual March Meet in Bakersfield. In one of the best races of the meet, McEwen put away the Swamp Rat with an 8.24 e.t. of 181.72 mph. *Photo courtesy of the scrapbook of Tom McEwen*

In 1964, at Fontana's Drag City, owner and driver Bob Johnson campaigned this full-bodied Junior Fuel dragster sponsored by B & L Auto Parts from San Diego, California. Byron Blair built the motor and Tom Hanna built the body. According to Tom Hanna, this was the only full-bodied Junior Fuel dragster that Hanna built. The small-block Dodge motor powered the nitro-burning dragster with Hilborn injectors. *Bob Thompson*

Doug Robinson makes the turn to the starting line in the Horsepower Engineering Top Fuel dragster at Fontana's Drag City drag strip. The yellow dragster featured an early Chrysler Hemi with a 6-71 GMC super-charger. *Bob Thompson*

# Memorable Moments of the 1960s
## Dennis Holding of "The Frantic Four"

*"At the New Jersey Raceway on August 1, 1964, we beat 'Big Daddy' Don Garlits in the final round becoming no. 1 in the 'Drag News Challenge' points meet for Top Eliminator"*

Driver Chuck Winsler, along with Jim Fox and Dennis Holding of "The Frantic Four," debuted this Modified Fuel roadster at Fontana's Drag City. Based on a Woody Gilmore chassis that was built at Race Car Engineering in Downey, California, the blown Chrysler 354 c.i. Hemi came right from a '56 Chrysler New Yorker that powered the roadster to 8.10 e.t.'s with speeds in of excess 190 mph. Cal Automotive built the metallic purple fiberglass body with a tapered tail section. *Bob Thompson*

Fontana's "Drag City" was home to some serious Top Fuel competition. Here, an unidentified Top Fuel dragster with a low profile Hilborn injector, mounted on top of an early Chrysler Hemi, blasts the quarter mile. *Bob Thompson*

Tom "The Mongoose" McEwen waits to blast down the quarter mile in the *Brand Motors Special*. Tom is fitted in his Simpson aluminized fire suit, gloves, boots, and the face mask in which Tom developed the breathing filters that keep out the noxious fumes of the fuels. Simpson built the mask to the U.S. Bureau of Mines safety standard. *Photo courtesy of the scrapbook of Tom McEwen*

The Top Fuel AA dragster of Porter, Chambers, and Ries lines up to blast down Drag City's quarter mile. Herb Ries drove the Southern California rocket to constant 7.80 e.t.'s - with speeds over 190 mph. *Bob Thompson*

At the K-Men Radio Drag Festival at Fontana, several local radio stations competed in sporting events pitted against others at the drags. K-Men from San Bernardino, California, sponsored the Top Fuel event with the entries of Lechein and Drake; the *Torkmaster* of Kenny Safford, Scotty's Muffler, Busby, and Westmoreland; and others. Here another dragster makes its way to the line. *Bob Thompson*

Jim Tice's Fontana Drag City, an American Hot Rod Association sanctioned track, was the first and only drag strip with an attending physician on site. Here another singshot makes a pass during the K-Men Radio Drag Festival. *Bob Thompson*

One of the most feared Top Fuel dragsters that ever traveled down the quarter mile was the Greer-Black-Prudhomme AA/FD. Tom Greer's machine shop sponsored the Keith Black-built Chrysler Hemi, and with the driving talents of Don Prudhomme, this team won over 80 percent of their races. Kent Fuller built the chassis for this national record-holding digger. In February 1963 Don ran the quickest time ever running a 7.77 e.t. of 190 mph. *Lou Hart*

The Huzoil-Horsepower Engineering Top Fuel dragster featured a 392 c.i. Chrysler Hemi, a George Britting body, and Mickey Thompson-equipped internal engine parts lubricated with Huzoil motor oil. Doug Robinson piloted the yellow fueler here at Fontana. *Bob Thompson*

Stars of American International's movie *Bikini Beach*, Frankie Avalon and Annette Funicello, check out Tommy Ivo's *Barnstormer* Top Fuel dragster during a break in filming. *Photo courtesy of the scrapbook of Tommy Ivo*

# Memorable Moments of the 1960s
## "T.V." Tommy Ivo

*"In 1964, during the filming of the movie* Bikini Beach, *Don Prudhomme and I were in a scene at the staring line with Don Rickles, who's character was 'Big Drag.' In order to shoot the scene without using a wide-angle lens, the scene was filmed with both cars in one lane. Don stood in-between the cars, with only a few feet separating them, as both cars came to life and staged. As Don raised and dropped the green flag, both cars launched with smoke billowing from the slicks and engulfed Don in a tremendous cloud. As Don emerged from the cloud, he couldn't hear, and he was covered with small bits of rubber. He walked up to the director, threw down his flag, and told him, 'I Quit!'"*

Tommy Ivo, with Keenan Wynn and Martha Hyer, break from *Bikini Beach* filming to discuss what it's like to go 200 mph with a supercharged Chrysler Hemi running on nitro. *Photo courtesy of the scrapbook of Tommy Ivo*

Don Rickles, aka "Big Drag," (right), takes a coffee break while leaning against T.V. Tommy Ivo's Top Fueler during the filming of *Bikini Beach*. The film was shot at Pomona Raceway. A mock-up of the Bikini Beach tower can be seen in the rear. *Photo courtesy of the scrapbook of Tommy Ivo*

Connie Kalitta's *Bounty Hunter* Top Fuel dragster at Riverside International Raceway in 1965. The blown 1957 Chrysler 392 Hemi was stroked to 400 c.i. The *Bounty Hunter* ran a 7.95 e.t. of 193 mph. *Bob Thompson*

During the 1960s drag racing pit crew members worked for the love of the sport and usually worked out of the back of pick-up trucks with simple hand tools. A typical team consisted of four to five guys having fun and working long hours for little money. Here's a Top Fuel team lifting up the rear of a dragster to change slicks with the use of a simple floor jack. *Bob Thompson*

Steve Swaja intensively checks the tune-up on the late Tony Nancy's *22 Jr.* Plymouth dragster at Riverside International Raceway. Steve designed several prominent dragsters throughout the Sixties. *Bob Thompson*

Mike Snivley, Tom McEwen, and John Mulligan share racing stories while Mulligan packs the chute during the 1968 Hot Rod Nationals at Riverside International Raceway. *Photo courtesy of the scrapbook of Tom McEwen*

At the 1965 *Hot Rod* Magazine's Nationals at Riverside International Raceway, the fuel pits were crowded with over 80 Top fuel dragsters attempting to qualify for the 32-car field. Here a Top Fuel team member awaits the command to report to the staging lanes. *Bob Thompson*

In 1965, Don "The Snake" Prudhomme took home honors by winning the NHRA Winternationals and the prestigious U.S. Nationals in Clermont, Indiana, driving Roland Leong's *Hawaiian* Top Fuel dragster. This was the first time in drag racing history that the Winternationals and Indy were won by the same car and driver in Top Fuel in the same year. *Photo courtesy of the scrapbook of Roland Leong*

The *Western Mfg. Special* AA/GD of Jon Halstead rolls to the staging lanes at Fremont Dragstrip in May 1965. The "Little Fuller"-built digger's blown small-block Chevy powered the short wheelbase dragster. The car has been restored in the San Francisco Bay area and is presently owned by Jim and Diane Laing. *James Handy*

Don Prudhomme (left) helps push the Greer-Black-Prudhomme Top Fuel dragster through the staging lanes at Fremont's Northern Nationals. One of the most dominant teams of the Sixties, the team won over 80 percent of their races. Shown here is the car without its nosepiece. *James Handy*

Roland Leong's Winternationals-winning *Hawaiian* Top Fuel dragster prepares to defeat the competition here at the 1966 March Meet at Bakersfield. The combination of drivers Mike Snively and Don Prudhomme gave the *Hawaiian* back-to-back victories at the U.S. Nationals at Indy later that year. *James Handy*

The pits at Fremont were busy with last-minute adjustments to either the motor or to make clutch changes. Here the blown Hilborn injected Chrysler Hemi gets new plugs and magneto work on the Capitol Speed Shop dragster. *James Handy*

Don Garlits and Emory Cook pose for photographer James Handy in the red painted Swamp Rat Top Fuel dragster at the March Meet in Bakersfield. The *Wynnscharger* featured the new 426 c.i. Dodge Hemi, a Tom Hanna-built body, and Joe Anderson applied the paint. Unfortunately it wasn't successful running a best 7.55 e.t. of 210 mph, so Don changed the color back to black. *James Handy*

At the 1965 Fuel & Gas Championships at Bakersfield, the *Chubasco* Top Fuel dragster of Jack Ewell, Bill Stecker, and Jim Kamboor featured a Kent Fuller chassis and a Steve Swaja-designed body. George Cerny painted the Jimmy Summers-formed body with Tony Nancy upholstery. Jack Ewell built the 475 c.i. blown Chrysler Hemi, and handled the driving chores. *James Handy*

The crew of John Peter's *Freight Train* gets the twin motored Chevrolet Top Gas dragster ready for their next round opponent at the March Meet in Bakersfield. The team won several "Best Appearing Crew" awards at national events for their uniforms. On one occasion, the *Freight Train* met up with the outlaw-dressed Billy "The Kid" Scott's crew. A shoot-out ensued on the starting line with cap guns blazing "The Great Train Robbery." *James Handy*

Tommy Ivo poses by his Kent Fuller bodied, Race Car Specialties–built, Top Fuel dragster known as *Chartruse* at the 1966 March Meet in Bakersfield. Tommy himself tuned the early 1957 392 Chrysler Hemi. *James Handy*

# Memorable Moments of the 1960s
## Roland Leong

*"My most memorable experience is when I crashed my first fuel car at Long Beach on its maiden voyage in 1964. I ran an 8:01 e.t. of 191 mph but I couldn't locate the parachute release and I ran off the left side of the track, hit the end sign, and ended up on the railroad tracks. The car was rebuilt, and with Don Prudhomme driving, won the 1965 NHRA Winternationals and the U.S. Nationals. In 1966, using the same car with the chassis lengthened and with new driver Mike Snively, we returned to the winner's circle at the NHRA Winternationals and the U.S Nationals. This was the first time any car had won both the Winternationals and the Indy U.S. Nationals in the same year!"*

Roland Leong tunes the Keith Black Hemi on his *Hawaiian* Top Fuel dragster. Roland struggled in his early match racing days but enjoyed success on the national level when Prudhomme and Snively drove for him in 1965 and 1966. *Photo courtesy of the scrapbook of Roland Leong*

In 1966, Roland Leong achieved drag racing history as his *Hawaiian* Top Fuel dragster, along with driver Mike Snively, recaptured the NHRA Winternationals and the U.S. Nationals again in the same year. *Photo courtesy of the scrapbook of Roland Leong*

"T.V." Tommy Ivo's *Giraffe* painted dragster had a Racecar Engineering chassis and a 392 c.i. Chrysler Hemi matched with a set of Doug's headers. Tommy and Tom McEwen toured the Hawaiian Islands for a series of match races and wowed the crowds. *Photo courtesy of the scrapbook of Tommy Ivo*

Sacramento Speed Shop owner Don Tognotti's beautiful streamlined dragster is seen here at Bakersfield in 1965. It was powered by a blown Chrysler Hemi. *James Handy*

At the 1966 Smokers March Meet in Bakersfield, a tough 64 Top Fuel field included the famous *Surfers* Top Fuel dragster of Bob Skinner, Tom Jobe, and driver Mike Sorokin. This dragster featured a 154-inch Race Car Specialties chassis and a 1957 Chrysler 392 c.i. Hemi running on 100 percent nitro. Tom Jobe readies to hand Sorokin his helmet prior to the final round where Sorokin defeated James Warren (in the other lane) running a 7.34 e.t. of 210 mph to win the event. *James Handy*

"Terrible" Ted Gotelli (left), from South San Francisco, cleans the Goodyears prior to making another pass during the 1966 March Meet at Bakersfield. Also shown are Tim Ryan, Dick Brohman, Lem Lemmelet, and driver Chuck Flores. *James Handy*

After years of running an unblown Chevrolet-powered dragster on fuel, the Logghe Brothers and driver Roy Steffey of Michigan brought their first Top Fuel dragster out to Fremont, California. It was dubbed *Slot Racer II*. The Logghe-built dragster was powered by an early Chrysler Hemi and driven by Maynard Rupp. *James Handy*

The shut down area at the end of Irwindale Raceway has a variety of dragsters. Here you can see Tom Larkin with his Top Gas dragster (left), a Junior Fueler, and another dragster powered by an early 392 c.i. Hemi, with the driver taking his helmet off. *Lou Hart*

Fresh from winning the 1968 AHRA Winternationals in Top Fuel the previous week, the Baney, Pink and Prud-homme dragster was renamed *Shelby's Super Snake* when Carroll Shelby became the full sponsor of the car. The Ed Pink-built 427 Ford SOHC "Cammer" powered the *Super Snake* to a 7.19 e.t., 217-mph pass to qualify in the 32 car field. Here, Ed Pink in the jacket (center), oversees the starting of the dragster. *Lou Hart*

The 1967 United States Professional Dragster Association Champion Don Prudhomme brings *Shelby's Super Snake* to life and adjusts his goggles to keep the nitro out of his eyes during the warm ups at the 1968 NHRA Winternationals. The 1,600-horsepower Ford "Cammer" powered Don to the third round where he was eventually defeated by Dwight Salisbury. *Lou Hart*

Running in the AHRA FX/T class, Fling Taylor's *US Turbine-1* featured a Turbonique engine, a Race Car Specialties chassis, and featured George "Stone-Age Man" Hutchinson behind the wheel. The Turbonique Drag axle engine produced 1,075 horsepower. It weighed only 120 pounds and had a length of 18 inches but kicked in a whopping 1,030 ft-lbs of torque at 7,200 rpm. *Lou Hart*

# Memorable Moments of the 1960s

## Jim Crooke

*"At Mission, British Columbia, with Jerry 'The King' driving, we made the first six second pass in the northwest posting a 6.79 et with a speed of 229 MPH."*

At the 1968 NHRA Winternationals, driver Bob Muravez, aka Floyd Lippencott, brings Jim Crooke's 427 SOHC Ford Top Fuel dragster *Assassin* to life. Jim, on the right wearing glasses, guides the Don Long built, Ed Pink powered digger through its warm ups. *James Handy*

Carlsbad Raceway featured the PDA Race of Champions where Don "The Snake" Prudhomme's *Shelby Super Snake* 427 SOHC Cammer, built by Ed Pink, squared off with his arch nemesis Tom "The Mongoose" McEwen's *Tirend Activity Booster* Top Fuel dragster. *Photo courtesy of the scrapbook of Tom McEwen*

"Starvin" Marvin Schwartz of Largo, Florida, owned the *Anaconda* Top Fuel dragster. Schwartz and Jim Marrone built the chassis, and Tom "Handy" Hanna built the aluminum body. George Cerney applied the paint. The 354 c.i. Chrysler Hemi was stroked to 398 c.i. and produced 7.20 e.t's with speeds above 216 mph. *Photo courtesy of the scrapbook of Lou Hart*

Tom "The Mongoose" McEwen, M&H Tire Company's Marvin Rifchen, and Don "The Snake" Prudhomme share a laugh on how Don lost to Tom by *this much. Photo courtesy of the scrapbook of Tom McEwen*

Jim Lynne at the wheel of Ted Gotelli's full-bodied dragster, which was featured in the infamous Coca-Cola advertisement in *LIFE* magazine. The 204-inch chassis built by Race Car Engineering nestled a 426 c.i. Chrysler Hemi for power. Ted rarely ventured outside of California to race but his name was well known throughout the racing world. *James Handy*

Jim Herbert's *The Lizard* Top Fuel dragster makes the turn to square up against the Champion Speed Shop entry during eliminations at the Fremont Top Fuel Championships. Fremont starter Chet Carter assists *The Lizard* to the starting line. Chet's infamous all-pink 1923 Ford Touring car can be seen in the background. *James Handy*

Tommy Ivo waits in the staging lane to qualify during the 1969 NHRA Winternationals at Pomona. John "Tarzan" Austin checks the magneto on the Keith Black Chrysler Hemi. *Lou Hart*

"Sneaky" Pete Robinson qualified strong with a 7.13 e.t. of 214.79 mph at the NHRA 1969 Winternationals at Pomona. Pete was a major force behind Ford's 427 c.i. SOHC Ford "Cammer" engine that produced nearly 1,600 horsepower. Facing Don Prudhomme in the first round, Pete red lighted giving the win to Don. *Arthur W. Bombay*

Dwight Salisbury in the Smothers Brothers-Beach Boys Top Fuel dragster was one of 82 dragsters that qualified fourth in the 32-car field, with a 7.08 e.t. of 225 mph. Dwight lost in the first round to Kenny Safford, in Ted Gotelli's car, running a quicker 7.17 e.t. of 213 mph to Kenny's 7.18 e.t. of 209 mph. *Arthur W. Bombay*

Minnesotan Tom Hoover's SOHC Ford-powered Top Fueler ran a 7.11 e.t. of 221 mph to qualify at the 1969 Winternationals. Tom gave Cliff Zink the first round win as Tom left too soon and red lighted. Note the oil filter protruding below the headers on the left side of the motor. *Arthur W. Bombay*

The Top Fuel dragster of Cerney-Manke-Lins featured a Don Long chassis and a 426 c.i. Chrysler Hemi, with Wes Cerney providing the power to run a 7.25 e.t. – of 221 mph at Pomona. Ron Manke handled the driving duties. *Arthur W. Bombay*

Don "The Snake" Prudhomme ran a 6.92 e.t. of 218.90 mph in his own *Wynn's Winder* Top Fuel dragster to take second place at the 1969 NHRA Winternationals. Prudhomme would eventually meet Beebe and Mulligan in the final round. *Arthur W. Bombay*

The 1969 Winternationals was a memorable one for Connie Kalitta and his *Bounty Hunter*. During Saturday's qualifying sessions, as Connie was being pushed down the fire-up road, the Boss 429 c.i. engine would not fire. The push car increased its speed and still the car would not fire. As the end of the fire-up road quickly approached, the car couldn't negotiate the turn and went through the fence, causing considerable front-end damage. Connie still made the field with an earlier 7.28 e.t. 209-mph pass. *Arthur W. Bombay*

Surveying the damaged Top
Fuel dragster of Connie Kalitta
was none other than Mickey
Thompson, and other race of-
ficials. Rumor has it that C. J.
"Pappy" was a mere few feet away
in a portable outhouse that was
nearly hit in the accident. *Arthur
W. Bombay*

During Sunday's first round eliminations, Connie Kalitta's repaired racecar faced off with Carl Olson in the Ewell-Bell-Olson entry, and defeated Chuck with a 7.13 e.t. of 189 mph but failed to return to the second round. *Arthur W. Bombay*

All the way from Rhode Island, Jimmy King (in the near lane) goes up in smoke against Don Cook's *South Wind Too* dragster, as Don ran a 7.22 e.t. of 209 mph to Jimmy's 7.48 e.t. of 212 mph. *Arthur W. Bombay*

The *Odd Couple* twin engine Top Gas dragster of Ken's Automotive smokes the tires during qualifying at the 1969 Winternationals. The combination of the big-block Chrysler Hemi mated to the small-block Chevy provided too much power on the Pomona asphalt in which the *Odd Couple* failed to qualify. *Arthur W. Bombay*

At the 1969 Winternationals Tom McEwen doubled up on his driving duties by shoeing his Top Fuel dragster and also his new Barracuda Funny Car. On the Top Fuel side, Tom failed to qualify but his Funny Car made the field. A first round upset win by Marv Eldridge put Tom out of the show. *Arthur W. Bombay*

# Memorable Moments of the 1960s
## Bob Muravez and Floyd Lippencott, Jr.

*"At Mickey Thompson's 200 Club Drag Race at Lions Drag Strip in 1966, driving Don 'The Beachcomer' Johnson's new Top Fuel dragster, we won the event over the Sandavol Brothers. The car was still primered and untested but there were nearly 80 dragsters at the event and we won top honors!"*

The "Monster of the Midway," the twin Chevrolet-powered *Freight Train* of John Peters with Bob Muravez behind the wheel, turned in a 7.81 e.t. of 175 mph at the 1969 Winternationals. The *Freight Train* received its name from Mickey Thompson's wife Trudy who heard the sounds the dragster made rumbling down the strip. *Arthur W. Bombay*

Al Bergler's beautiful new BB/GD debuted at the 1969 Winternationals. The Logghe Brothers built the chassis, and an early Chrysler Hemi supplied the power with Al doing the metal work. Here Al runs an 8.38 e.t. of 149.50 mph against the *Hot Sauce* dragster. *Arthur W. Bombay*

Super Eliminator class at the 1969 Winternationals had the Junior Fuelers of Fred Kramer driving the Gustin-Kramer-Sterns out in front of Don Enriquez in the Adams and Enriquez injected Hemi dragster. *Arthur W. Bombay*

A Southern California favorite, Walt Rhodes in the Gas House Gang's AA/GD blistered the Pomona asphalt running a 7.64 e.t. of 198 mph during qualifying at the Winternationals. Rhodes took out Mike Snively in the first round but hung a red light against Bowers and Smith in the next round. *Arthur W. Bombay*

In the final round at the 1969 NHRA Winternationals, John "The Zookeeper" Mulligan in the Beebe and Mulligan entry faced Don Prudhomme's *Wynn's Winder* and put away "The Snake," as Don experienced engine woes. John turned in a 6.95 e.t. of 211.38 mph. *Arthur W. Bombay*

Kansas' John Wiebe lifts the front wheels during qualifying at the 1969 All Pro Series season opener at Orange County International Raceway. Roy Fjastad's Speed Products Engineering built the racecar. It was later the first front-motor car to receive an Ed Donovan aluminum Hemi. John ran consistent 6.80 e.t.'s of 215-plus mph. *James Handy*

Don Prudhomme's *Wynn's Winder* Top Fuel dragster ran three sub-seven second passes during the finale of the 1969 All Pro Series at Orange County International Raceway. Prudhomme, of Granada Hills, California, ran a 6.84 e.t. of 220 mph to defeat Steve Carbone in the final round. Prudhomme also won the U.S Nationals at Indy later that year. *James Handy*

Hayward, California's Gary Ritter drove the Ritter, Kinner, and Carey's *Blood, Sweat & Nitro* Top Fuel dragster, shown here at Orange County International Raceway's PDA Meet. The Northern California gang combined efforts to run 6.70 e.t.'s of 220 mph throughout the event. *James Handy*

Dwight Hughes piloted the Berry Brothers and Hughes Top Fuel dragster at the Hotwheel Nationals at Fremont, California. Dwight defeated the likes of Ron Hampshire and Dennis Baca while running consistent 6.80 e.t.'s of 215 mph. *James Handy*

The *Renegade* Top Fuel dragster of "Chassis" John Shoemaker was driven by the late Gary Ormsby, Sr. Shoemaker, of Sacramento, California, terrorized the northwest circuit defeating some of the big names in racing. The *Renegade* is shown here at Fremont's Northern Nationals. *James Handy*

Jesse Perkins' *Cow Palace Shell* Top Fuel dragster reigned from Northern California. Rich Bruckman "drops the laundry" after completing a 6.90 e.t., 196-mph pass here at Fremont's Northern Nationals. *James Handy*

Rick Ramsey in the *California Charger* of Keeling and Clayton defeats the team of Bill Wishart and "Wild" Bill Alexander in this classic battle at Fremont. Ramsey ran a blistering 6.53 e.t. of 218 mph to Alexander's 7.08 e.t. of 184 mph at the Hot Wheels Northern Nationals. *James Handy*

Steve "Mandrill" Carbone completes a pass in the Creitz and Greer Top Fuel dragster, from Tulsa, Oklahoma. The beautiful blue fueler featured a 426 c.i. Dodge Hemi fitted with a 6-71 GMC Supercharger. The popular team ran consistent 6.70 e.t.'s with speeds over 215 mph. *James Handy*

Jerry "The King" Ruth, hailing from the Pacific Northwest, lights up the Goodyears here at the 1969 PDA Meet at Orange County International Raceway. The *Pay n Pac* relied on a 392 c.i. Chrysler Hemi for power. *James Handy*

Kenny Safford in the newly unpainted Gotelli's Speed Shop Top Fuel dragster from San Francisco. Kenny qualified "Terrible" Ted's entry with a 6.902 e.t. at the 1971 NHRA Winternationals at Pomona. Kenny made it all the way to the finals where he defeated Jim King in the semifinals with a 6.85 e.t., 217-mph run. Eventually, mechanical problems forced him out of the final round against Don Garlits' new rear engine dragster. *Bob Thompson*

Dick Rosberg lights up the Goodyears in Mike Kuhl's Top Fuel dragster at the Hot Wheels Northern Nationals at Fremont. The RCS-built digger featured a 392 Chrysler Hemi built with Arias engine parts, Jardine headers, an Engle camshaft, and a Hays clutch. *James Handy*

Mike Snively returned to the Top Fuel ranks driving Don Prudhomme's "Hot Wheels" Top Fuel dragster at Fremont's Northern Nationals. Snively dominated the field running 6.56 e.t.'s of 222.22 mph, stopping Rick Ramsey in the finals. *James Handy*

Larry Huff's *Soapy Sales* Top Fuel dragster, with veteran Steve Carbone behind the wheel, gets the front wheels out of the groove at Fremont. Huff also campaigned a Top Fuel Funny Car and a Pro Stock Dodge. *James Handy*

The other half of the Wildlife team was Tom "Mongoose" McEwen's "Hot Wheels" Top Fuel dragster. Tom's *Mongoose I* featured a Ramchargers-built 426 Chrysler Hemi and Simpson safety equipment. At the Bakersfield March Meet, Tom missed the bump for Top Fuel, but drove his "Hot Wheels" Plymouth Duster Funny Car to the second round. *James Handy*

During Friday's qualifying at the 1971 March Meet at Bakersfield, Jim Davis, a chassis builder from Walnut Creek, California, blasted out a 6.95 e.t., only to grenade the entire left side of the 354 c.i. Chrysler Hemi. Jim singed his eyes with fire being fueled by hot oil spewing from the motor, and the dragster received extensive damage to the fire boot, upholstery, and chute packs. Davis and his crew prepped the car to run again on Saturday with another powerplant. While the traction on the track greatly improved, the power on the track proved disastrous. This sequence of photos shows that Davis experienced a mid-track wheel stand that resulted in a backward flip and ended with numerous spectacular rolls. Davis received a badly broken arm and destroyed his racecar. *James Handy*

The late Tony Nancy, of Sherman Oaks, California, captured the Top Fuel crown at the 12th Annual March Meet at Bakersfield, defeating Harry Hibler in the final round. Hibler made a strong showing throughout the meet, but he red lighted his chances away. The "Loner" tackled his way through a tough 32-car field to collect the $6,000 First Place prize money. *James Handy*

James Warren ran a 8.53 e.t. of 143.50 mph while throwing a rod out of the bottom of the Chrysler Hemi in the Warren-Coburn-Miller Top Fuel dragster at the 1970 NHRA March Meet at Bakersfield. James advanced three rounds but eventually lost to winner Tony Nancy by running a 7.17 e.t. of 209 mph to Nancy's 7.03 e.t. of 217 mph. *Bob Thompson*

Tommy Ivo blasts through the lights at a 6.99 e.t. of 204 mph at the 12th Fuel & Gas Champions Meet at Bakersfield. Tommy's first round loss was at the hands of low event qualifier Norm Wilcox. *Bob Thompson*

The *American Bandstand* Top Fuel dragster at the 12th Annual Smokers March Meet at Famoso Dragstrip. Rod Dunn qualified the *Bandstand* with a strong 7.01 e.t., but the digger lost fire in the first round against Jim Dunn. *Bob Thompson*

Red Fogleman's *Odd Couple* AA/GD unloads the laundry at the 12th Annual March Meet at Bakersfield. The combination of Fogleman's small-block Chevy/big-block Chrysler Hemi produced 7.70 e.t.'s of 209 mph. The *Couple* lost to the other twin–motored monster, the *Freight Train*, in the semifinals. *Bob Thompson*

The Keeling, Clayton and Ramsey's beautiful *California Charger* made it to the finals at the 13th March Meet in Bakersfield. Rick defeated Warren-Coburn-Miller, and Larry Dixon, but lost to Don Garlits' new rear-engine dragster on a hole shot in the final round. Rick ran a quicker 6.64 to Don's 6.71 e.t. *James Handy*

Norm Wilcox behind the wheel of Ted Gotelli's San Francisco based new Top Fueler here at Sears Point Raceway in 1971. Gotelli's Speed Shop dragsters were always wreaking havoc on the West Coast. Gotelli's dragster was low qualifier with a 6.70 e.t., 213-mph pass at the 1971 Winternationals. *James Handy*

Tom "The Mongoose" McEwen cracks a 6.80 e.t., 212-mph pass down Parker Ave. in his Mattel "Hot Wheels" Top Fueler at the 1971 Winternationals. The Ramchargers-built 426 Chrysler Hemi provided the power behind McEwen's team cars. *James Handy*

Billy Tidwell in the Critz and Donovan Top Fuel dragster smokes the Goodyears during qualifying. The Ramchargers Donovan Engineering-built engine featured a different air intake mounted on top of the injector. *James Handy*

Rick Ramsey powers the entry of Keeling and Clayton's *California Charger* past Larry Dixon during eliminations at the Bakersfield March Meet. Ramsey also pulled double-duty driving the Keeling and Clayton *California Charger* Ford Pinto Funny Car during the same event. *James Handy*

After this 200-plus mph run, this unidentified dragster literally had the front wheels off the ground when the chute deployed here in the lights at Fremont Dragstrip. *James Handy*

Fresh off a victory at the 11th Annual NHRA Winternationals just weeks before, Walt Stevens drove the *Odd Couple* AA/GD to the winner's circle at the 13th Annual Fuel & Gas Championships at Bakersfield. The Ken's Automotive Engineering sponsored dragster dumped Ken Moitza in the final round. *James Handy*

Two of the most influential drag racing legends that traveled down the quarter mile were "Big Daddy" Don Garlits and Don "The Snake" Prudhomme. Their contributions and achievements to the sport of drag racing are too numerous to list. These legends established, and broke, nearly every drag racing record throughout the 1960s and 1970s. Here they both exchange "bench racing" stories prior to going head-to-head at OCIR. *Steve Delgadillo*

# Memorable Moments of the 1960s

## "Big Daddy" Don Garlits

*"My most memorable moment in the '60s was at Half Moon Bay Dragstrip in California. In 1966,* Drag Racing Magazine *hosted an event to determine who was the best in the USA. It came down to Don Prudhomme and myself. It was a two out of three match. A very large trophy was to be given to the winner and a much smaller one to the runner up. I won the race, and when the presentation took place they had to remove the Snake's name from the big trophy and put my name from the small trophy in its place. I enjoyed it that much better than the win. The Californians were so sure that I would lose! I was so excited that I drove nearly back to L.A. before I realized that I had left the facility without getting paid! I drove back and Smith was waiting with my money. It was a large payday and I still have the big trophy with the funny brass plate with my name on it."*

Don Garlits piloted his restored *Swamp Rat VI*, the same car he drove in 1964 on his way to the first of his eight drag racing titles. *Lou Hart*

Don Garlits' rear engine dragster changed the history of drag racing when he debuted this mid-engine Top Fuel dragster in 1971. Don's success to construct and build a safe but competitive dragster changed the history of drag racing as Don dominated the 11th Annual NHRA Winternationals, the March Meet Fuel & Gas Championships at Bakersfield, the NHRA Springnationals, and was named *Drag News* Top Fuel Driver of the Year for 1971. *James Handy*